*I'm In My Feelings Series*

## OTHER BOOKS BY ROBERT M. DRAKE

Spaceship (2012)
The Great Artist (2012)
Science (2013)
Beautiful Chaos (2014)
Beautiful Chaos 2 (2014)
Black Butterfly (2015)
A Brilliant Madness (2015)
Beautiful and Damned (2016)
Broken Flowers (2016)
Gravity: A Novel (2017)
Star Theory (2017)
Chaos Theory (2017)
Light Theory (2017)
Moon Theory (2017)
Dead Pop Art (2017)
Chasing The Gloom: A Novel (2017)
Moon Matrix (2018)
Seeds of Wrath (2018)
Dawn of Mayhem (2018)
The King is Dead (2018)
What I Feel When I Don't Want To Feel (2019)
What I Say To Myself When I Need To Calm The
Fuck Down (2019)
What I Say When I'm Not Saying A Damn Thing
(2019)
What I Mean When I Say Miss You, Love You &
Fuck You (2019)

**For Excerpts and Updates please follow:**

Instagram.com/rmdrk
Facebook.com/rmdrk
Twitter.com/rmdrk

*ISBN: 978-1-7326900-6-6*

Book Cover: Robert M. Drake

*For The Ones Who Feel A Little More*

# CONTENTS

# What I Mean When I Say Miss You, Love You & Fuck You

ROBERT M. DRAKE

## AFTER TOMORROW

In the end,
we always have

something to lose.

Something we regret.

That's life.

We anticipate so much.

Some that happen

and some
that never reach the shore.

That never reach us
when we need them most.

And for what?
To live for a moment?

To believe in something
or have something

to keep you going.

It is all for a reason.

All for hope
and love.

For something,
anything,
to hold on to.

To take with you
as time goes on.

I have learned,
in all my years,

that

in the end,
that is what we live for.

The little moments.
The little victories.

Whether we keep them
or not.

## LESSONS

The best lesson
you can ever give someone

is

the realization
of self-love.

And that alone
is the most

valuable lesson
in the world.

## I AM NOT SCARED

You do not
terrify me.

You give me strength.

And I'm asking you
to love me

when I am falling apart.

When I have nothing left
to give.

And when I am broken down
to the smallest parts of myself.

That is all.
Nothing major.

To love me
and leave nothing

behind.

To love me
and

celebrate what we have

until our bones
are the only thing

left.

## IF THEY

If they love you,

they'll make the effort.

They'll be there for you
when you need them most.

They'll try to understand you
even when they don't see

eye to eye with you.

They'll support you
no matter what—in anything
you wish to chase.

They'll correct you
when you're wrong.

Teach you
when you need guidance.

Lead you
when you feel lost

and let you move on

when you're ready

to be on your own.

If they love you,
they'll set you free,

but never quite
stop looking out for you.

No matter what happens.
No matter how far you go.

Lovers come in
and out of our lives

but true friendship
is hard to come by.

Hard to forget.

And

even harder
to let go.

*Remember this.*

## THE POSIBILITY

Everything and anything
is possible

when you open your heart.

When you
open yourself

to everything that hurts.

This is where
you will unlock

what truly matters.

Where you will find
the kind of love

that will keep your heart
young forever.

That will keep your
soul on fire.

## DESERVE

We deserve
some kind of love.

Soft and gentle.
Fun and sad.

But never haunting
when it leaves.

We all deserve
some kind of love.

As long as we are ready
to let it go.

As long as we know
nothing is forever.

*Everything has its place.*

Its rightful moment
to exist

and disappear.

From you
to me.

The clock is
always ticking.

## NOTHING LEFT

There is nothing left
for you to hurt.

Nothing left
to bury.

Or kill.
Or label.
Or misconstrue.

My world has ended
many times before.

But it has also
begun.

*I am endless.*

And everyday
I am different.

And you can try
to hold me back.

Break me down.
Destroy me

or hate me.

But like the shoreline,

I will always come back.

Always return stronger
and kinder.

Tougher
and softer.

This is the way I heal.

The way I live
and survive.

This is the way I love.

And there is
nothing you can do

to change that.

## LOVE MORE PLEASE

Love more.
Let it be religion.

Give in to it.

Let it defeat you
but not destroy you.

Let it define you
but not control you.

Let it fill you
but not empty you.

Love more.
Doubt less.

Love more.
Fear less.

Feel more.
Criticize less—hate less.

Stand for something.
Fall for nothing.

*Let it be religion.*

Praise what you
hold within.

Then release it
to the world.

There is so much
to live for.

So much to do
and abide for.

Don't ever lose
sight of this:

There are so many
reasons to die for.

Let love
be one of them.

## SAY A WORD

We didn't have
to say a word.

We didn't have
to do

all of those things

we thought
we had to do

for each other
to show each other

we cared.

That we loved.

That we wanted to be
a part of each other's lives.

We didn't do
any of that.

We just knew.

And it was
the kind of knowing

we didn't have
to reassure.

We didn't have
to prove.

*We just knew.*

From the moment we met.

*We knew.*

It was
that kind of love.

That kind
of connection

and it was

the kind
that moved

*the soul.*

## STORIES

You tell stories
that only

I can relate to.

That only
I can feel.

*This is why I love you.*

I see myself in you.
I feel a piece

of what I love

*bloom*

out of your soul.

## NO EARS HERE

You stop apologizing
for yourself

the moment you realize
what you feel.

What you know.
What you are.

And that

*YOU ARE*

of your own creation

and not
of the work of others.

Not the work
of anyone

but yourself.

You are responsible
for what

you put out.

What you put
into your soul.

No one
owes you anything.

And you don't
owea damn thing

to anyone.

Your life
is your life.

Stop apologizing
for what you are.

Become
who you want

to become.

Offend
who you want

to offend
while doing so.

The world
doesn't give you mercy

and neither should you.

*Be fierce.*
*Be strong.*
*Be unapologetic.*

Find your place.

Accept
and love yourself

for who you are.

It is more terrifying
to be

and do less.

It is a waste
to try and

go against yourself.

To make yourself

believe
you are a wave,

when indeed,

you are

very much
like an ocean.

Stay Beautiful,
my friends.

## STRONG WOMEN

A strong woman
is a dangerous thing

to the careless man.

She knows her place.

She knows
what she feels

and she is confident
in her thoughts.

Her voice is a dagger
and her heart

is the fire
that cast it.

This I say

to all the young men
who take advantage

of them.

*Beware of them.*

For they are everywhere.
And together

they are indestructible.

They are strong enough
to conquer

the world.

To heal
the world.

And rid it
of the bullshit

*weak men bring.*

## TYPE OF THINGS

We have to meet
in the middle

if we want it
to work.

You have your things
you have to let go of

and so do I.

And it's not
going to be easy.

Because these type of things

never are.

But we want each other
and we have

to start somewhere.

And I know
deep within our hearts,

we want to believe
in the possibility

of love.

We want to believe
in the capacity of it.

And we want to accept it
at all cost.

But we have to meet
in the middle of it all.

In the center
of where

it hurts.

# BURY YOUR HEART

You have to bury
your feet

in the sand
before you can stand.

Before you can stretch
your arms

toward the sky
and kiss the clouds.

Bloom straight
toward the sun,

my sweet, little love.

You're a flower.

You deserve all the space
you need.

As long
as it helps you grow.

## A WAY OUT

There's always a way out.

Always a speck of light
somewhere.

If anyone out there
is struggling with something

or someone,

*know*
that there is always

a way.

Always
someone to talk to.

Always someone
to guide you

toward safety.

*Know*
that there are always options.

That there are always
several different

choices
and outcomes.

*Know*
that you don't have to

go through this alone.

That you don't have to
close yourself up either.

There's always someone
willing to help you.

Someone willing to listen
and pull you back

to where you belong.

There is both good
and bad in the world.

Both dark and light.

And you should always
choose the light.

The light in moments.
The light in decisions.
And the light in people.

Always.

*ALWAYS*

*keep this*
*in the back of*

*your mind*
*and heart.*

## FEEL IT

Your heart
is going to believe

what it wants
to believe.

Love
who it wants
to love.

No matter how many times
it has been broken.

It will believe anything
to feel happiness.

*To feel a little ease.*
*A little comfort.*

This is the curse
of being human.

You love
who you love

no matter how many times
they've hurt you.

You will always

give them
the best parts
of you.

*No matter what.*

## HAD I KNOWN

If I had known
this was the last time

I would have
seen you...

then I would have
held you

a little longer.

I would have told you
the things

I've been carrying
in my chest.

I would have stayed
with you

throughout the night.

I would have tried
to save you.

I would have
listened to you.

I would have put
my pride

and ego aside.

And I would have
loved you

for as long
as I could have.

If only
I had known.

But now
*it's too late.*

Life's a bitch sometimes.

It gives
when you're not ready

and it takes away
the moment

you realize
its worth.

## WHAT MATTERS

Everything about you
matters.

So who are you
to tell yourself

you're not special.

You are loved
and sometimes

that's enough.

## PEOPLE COME

People come
and go.

And I think
we both know this.

We both understand it.

And this is why
we don't get along.

This is why
we can't seem

to get it together.

Because deep down inside,
*we know*

we are doomed
from the start.

And we want
things to work

but ultimately,

*we know* they won't.

We know
what we have

is temporary.

And that's

what hurts
the most.

## WHAT CHANGES

People rarely
ever change

and when they do,

they do it
because

they have no other choice.

They ultimately
do it

for themselves.

## BUMPED INTO

You've got to wonder
how many people

you have had the chance
to get to know

but didn't.

How many people
you could have loved

but never had

the opportunity
to do so.

Out of all the people
you've bumped into

out in public
by mistake.

Passed while crossing
the street

or been behind
in a grocery store line.

*Imagine…*

the incredible
loss of possibility here.

The possible loss
of love.

Of companionship.

Sometimes
we live our lives waiting.

Thinking.
Believing.

That the people
around us,

close to us,
are all we have.

But we are wrong.
So wrong.

We don't take enough
chances.

We don't take
enough time.

And we don't think
of the possibility.

Perhaps
we deserve more

but little
do we believe it.

We are blinded by
our own reality.

By our own perception
of what we think

*love is.*

So much,
that we don't know

any better.

The love of your life
could be passing

you by

and sadly,

you will do nothing
about it.

And that is all
I have to say

about that.

## BROKEN INSIDE

Of course
you're going to say

that you are attracted
to broken people.

That you are drawn
to them

because that's how you
feel inside.

But in all honesty,
we are all

a bit broken inside.

We are all
a bit sad

and have a bit
of a tortured past.

I've never met anyone
who has yet

to endure pain.

Anyone
who hasn't had

their heart broken.

This is why
we see ourselves

in the empty.

In the lost
and broken.

In the confused,
in the unordinary

and out of place.

It is because
we all carry this within.

Everyone has
a sad story

to tell

and everyone has
a little pain

hidden somewhere.

A scar

*waiting*

to be read.

A heart

*waiting*

to be understood.

## TRUST IS HARD

I want to trust you.

I want to believe
in what you have to offer.

Even if I know
it is nothing.

I want to love you.
I really do.

This is how I am.

I over-think things
even if it is all

in my head.

I believe
even if it is not real.

I love
even if you have nothing

to offer.

This is my curse
and mine alone.

To put myself
through so much pain

even if
it does not exist.

I must be mad.

Or I must be
in love.

*You decide.*

## WANT YOU

How could I not
want you.

With a heart like that.

You make me
want to spend

the rest of my life
with you.

## MYSELF

I leave pieces
of myself

in all
the things I love.

Maybe that is why
I feel

so goddamn
empty sometimes.

Maybe

that is why
I feel lost.

I risk myself
to save others

and in the end,

I barely recognize
who I am.

This is
the only way

I know

how to love.

## SOMEONE TO LOVE

If you have
someone to love,

love them.
And love them well.

There are too many
people starved

or deprived of it.

Everyone deserves
someone to smile about.

Someone beautiful enough
to stay.

## YOU AND I

Everyone feels
like an empty house

*sometimes.*

# IN DARKNESS

Yes.
It is true.

Beautiful things
do emerge

from broken things.

Flowers do grow
in concert.

Light does shimmer
in darkness.

And love
is found

in the most
unusual of places.

Hope is a beautiful thing.

All you have to do
is believe.

## WHAT I LEARNED

You let me go
without an explanation.

And left methere
feeling like the rain

and wanting to die.

And after all these years,
the only thing

I have learned

is...

how letting go
has no rules.

How good-byes
come without warning.

And how no one
owes you anything,

not even
if you have
given them

*all*

that you are.

## STILL KILLS ME

Maybe I left
who I once was

with you.

Maybe you still
have my heart

and maybe
it still hurts.

Maybe I was
that one flower

you fell
in love with.

The one you had
to have

had to clip
from its roots—

to take home.

And maybe
you had no idea

what to do with me.

Maybe you just left me
out here to die.

After a few months
of giving you joy.

You gave me darkness
instead of light.

You yanked me
out of

what I knew.

And now,
it is too late

to go back
to the way

things were.

*Before you destroyed
the peace
I once had.*

## THE ONLY THING

Sometimes a long talk
is what you need.

Sometimes it is
the only thing

that can heal you.

Someone to listen to you
while you pour out

your heart.

Someone
to be there for you

when you feel the urge
to break apart.

A conversation
is a beautiful thing.

It can pull you out
of the darkness

when nothing
else can.

## MEMORY

It is a tragedy

that we could not
make it work.

That we could not
find it

within ourselves
to stay.

It is sad to believe
but the last memory

of you,
of us,

was spent
in silence.

In ways
to explain

what we really
wanted

but did not

have the courage
to say.

## DISCOVERING

When you find yourself.

When you learn
that the opinions of others

do not matter.

When you laugh
with your friends.

When you find
the love of your life.

When you discover
your purpose.

And when you're
genuinely happy.

That's everything.
That's beautiful.

Hold it
for as long

as you
must.

## ONE MOMENT

It is about
that one moment

when you finally love

yourself
and realize

what you deserve.

That alone
changes everything.

That alone
makes all the difference.

## ONE DAY

Maybe one day
we'll meet again

and explain
to each other

what really happened.

Maybe one day
we'll finally understand.

Until then,
I hope you live

your best life.

And I hope
you really do

all things
you always said

you wanted
to do.

## I WONDER

I wonder
if you miss me

when I miss you.

Think of me
when I think of you.

It hurts to say,
but sometimes

I wonder
if you feel me

the same way
you felt me

when we were
in love.

The same way
you felt me

when we were
together.

*Nothing has changed.*

At least,

not for me.

## FIND YOU FIND ME

Love can be found
anywhere

and that alone
should be inspiring

enough
to look for it.

To find it
in the most unusual

of places.

To let it
find you

when you're not
expecting it

at all.

Keep your heart open.

You never know
what's meant for you.

You never know

how much love

you're meant
to receive.

## LOVE AGAIN

What good is love
if it is not shared.

What good
is the fire

within your soul
if you do not

let others
feel it.

*Learn to love again.*

And again.
And again.

No matter
how many times
you've been broken.

There is always more.
*Enough.*

Without fear of loss.
Love freely.

It is,

without a doubt,

worth living for.
Worth every moment

of sadness.
And pain.

And laughter.
And joy.

Just share
what you feel within.

*Know it.*

And do it now.
Nothing is forever.

At some point,
everything is lost

but nothing
is forgotten.

## NEVER IS

You've been sad
and heartbroken.

Of course you have.

But you have also
healed and learned.

You have also
risen and grown.

It is not the end.
It never is.

The sun rises.
The moon rises.

And somewhere
in-between,

there is light
and there is

you.

## EXPECT THEM TO

No one knows
when or how

or even why
but the right people

always find you
when you

need them most.

And they always appear
when you least

expect them to.

*Understand.*

Love is love.

No matter where
it comes from.

Who
it comes from.

Keep your heart open.

The right person
will find you

and at
the right moment.

*I promise.*

## IN A JAR

Not everyone
is going to value you.

Some people
will watch

the flowers grow.

They will admire them
in their own space.

While others
will pick them.

They will put them
in a jar

and watch
them dry.

Know the difference.
Know your worth.

And walk with those
who give you life.

Not death.

It is your turn
to heal.

To grow.
To reach the sky.

To feel the rain
and stand on your own.

*Be your own flower.*

And protect
your heart

at all cost.

## REMEMBER THIS

Do not
hate them

for burdening you
with pain

and sadness.

Forgive them.
Make peace with them.

Feel the wind.
It changes.

It moves on.
And it does not stop

for anyone.

Remember this.

## YOU HURT

Maybe you are sensitive
because you hurt

the way you hurt.

But that doesn't
make you weak.

You've outlasted
the pain

and you've outgrown
so much.

You're a lot
stronger than you think.

You're a rose
lifted by thorns.

A star
born of chaos.

And the feeling
of love

in a world
full of hate.

You're beautiful, baby.

Don't let
anyone

rob you
of your light.

## WHAT IS MISSING

I hope you find
what's missing

and I hope
you fill that void

that has always
haunted you.

I hope you find it
within yourself

to move on.

I hope you find
the strength you need

to take
one step forward—even

if you're exhausted.

I hope you find
someone

who can make you
smile.

Someone
who could make you

laugh.

Especially
in this dark,

cold world.

I hope you accept
failure

and I hope
you learn as much

as you can
from them.

I hope gentle good-byes
find you

and I hope
you meet beautiful people

along your way.

I hope you learn
to forgive yourself

and I hope

you find a way

to find peace.

As for me,
I will continue

to think
about you.

And I will continue
to smile.

I will continue
to live

my best life.

I hope these words
find you,

even if they're not
from me.

And I hope
they remind you

to keep going—to
never give up

on yourself

or

on your dreams.

Stay beautiful, baby.

I will miss you.

## SOMETIMES

Sometimes I feel
like the only reason

you stay
is because

you've invested
so much of your time

in me.

It's sad,
I know,

but there's no other way
to put it.

You don't have to
if you don't want to.

I'll be okay
on my own.

I just hope
you find the happiness

you deserve.

## MY FAVORITE

You will always
be

my favorite.

No matter who
I meet

or who
I fall in love with.

You will always be
*the one*

who got away.

The one
I breathe to love.

The one
I'll always regret

letting go.

## LETTING GO

There is nothing scary
about letting go.

What is scary
is holding on

while knowing
you have nothing left

to give.

Nothing left
to receive.

And that's a hard choice
to do.

Especially
when it's

with someone
you love.

## PERHAPS

If you only knew
what I felt.

If you only knew
what I've been through.

Then perhaps,
things would be different.

Perhaps,
you'd want to

rescue me

rather than
leave me.

Make me
your own

instead

of letting
me go.

## CHOICES

Your ability
to choose

who you let in
is a gift.

One
of the most

important choices
to make.

Never forget
this power.

When it comes
to matters of the heart,

it's all
you need

to know.

## STONES BREAK

Only a heart
made of stone breaks.

Only a heart
that hasn't been

handled
with care.

Stay soft, my friends.

## THE DEEP END

Your friends
will always

bring you back
toward the light.

They will always
pull you out

of the deep end.

*Be kind to them.*

Because friend
is another word

for family

and family
does not

let their own drown.

Does not
let their own

go

too far
off the deep end.

They will always
keep an eye on you.

Even when
you think

no one is looking.

## YOU ASKED ME

And you asked me
why people let go.

Why people leave
without a proper

good-bye.

And I told you
they do it

to move on.

They do it
to test themselves.

To see
if that's

what they really want.

And that's okay.

Sometimes
people have no choice

but to let go...

in order to heal.
To grow.

To learn to appreciate
the people they have.

Sometimes
people let go
to see

if that's
what they *really*

deserve.

## STRANGERS

You were
a stranger once.

Someone
I only dreamed of.

And now
you're just someone

I used to know.

And sadly,
you were the one

who went away
but also,

*the one*

who was telling me
not to go.

# I SHOULD HAVE NOT

I know
I should have.

But I have not
changed my number

since you left.

And I haven't
just in case

you find
the courage within you

to call—to

text me
one day

out of the blue.

I know
a lot has changed

but I'd still
like to hear from you.

I'd still

like to be your friend.

I don't know
where you are

or how to reach you

*but*

maybe one day
we'll laugh

over the tragedy
we caused each other.

Maybe one day
we'll make sense

of the aching pain
we left behind.

Maybe one day,
right?

Until then,
we're only

a phone call away.

A text message
from sharing

what we really
feel.

## WALK AWAY

You don't awaken
someone's love

and leave them.

You just don't
bring out the best

in people
and walk away

the moment
you make them feel

something real.

## OVERTHINKING

You go home
thinking about

what hurts.

Thinking about
what you could have

done.

About why it happened
the way it happened.

It never ends.

And you will
over-think it,

over
and over again.

But it won't
change anything.

The only thing
that will change

is your perception.

Everything else
stays with you.

Every scar
will always

hold

a special place
in your heart.

A special moment.
A special memory.

Regardless
if it hurts

or not.

## I AM SORRY

And I lied
to you

that last night
we spoke.

And it was
the first

and only time
I ever lied

to you.

Because

you asked me
if I was going

to be okay
and still,

I swallowed my heart
and said

I would be fine...

when really

all I wanted to do

was lay
within your arms.

## YOUR FIGHT

I know you have
a lot on your mind—in

your heart.

And I also know
we have a lot of things

to celebrate
and mourn over.

But let us not
forget

how much
we need one another.

Let us not forget
how far

we've come.

How much
we've grown.

How much
we've learned
to let go.

Let us remember,
at least for a moment,

that we still have
each other.

That we're still here
fighting against the odds.

Making sense
of what terribly

hurts… together.

Let us remember
that our friendship

has never been
stronger than now.

That we still have
this moment

and that
we should always use it
to live,

but also,
to love.

## HAUNTS ME

I know you think
you took everything

about you
away from me.

But the truth is,
something remained.

And I can't recall
what it is.

I can't even touch
or see it

but I know
it is there.

And it's hard for me
to fathom

because

I asked myself
how could I

want your love back.
How could I feel

as if

I need it
to survive.

How could I miss

something

that never existed.

Dream of a place
I never visited.

Or fall in love
with a person

I never knew.

It's hard to believe.

For you,
maybe it was

just a fling,
but to me

it was god
creating the universe.

A flash of light

that barely killed me.

A kiss
that has haunted me
ever since.

One I have yet
to recover from.

One I have yet
to forget.

## WE MUST

We must always
remember

how all endings
are also

beginnings.

How when you lose
someone

it only means
you're making room

for someone new.

So don't be afraid,
everything will sort itself out

for the best.

Always

welcome the beginning
of things.

## UNFORGETABLE

One day,
you will make sense

of all these questions
and you will know

exactly
why it happened.

Why it hurt
and why

*it was*
*unforgettable.*

## LIFE IS STRANGE

Life is strange.

As soon
as you stop wanting

something,
you get it,

and as soon
as you realize

what you want,

life makes it
impossible to obtain.

*Life is hard.*

We barely get
what we need

and we barely know
what we deserve.

## THE SKY

The darker the sky,
the more real

it gets.

Some nights
I miss you

more than others
and some nights

I'm afraid
of what

you make
me feel.

## LONGER HERE

Getting over someone
is hard.

You have to pretend
you're okay.

You have to act
like you don't care

and above all,

you have to erase
what you once loved

for what
no longer

is there.

## WHAT YOU KNEW

Things you once knew.

People you once loved.
Things you miss.

Love doesn't change,
you change,

and time
can either make you

thankful
or regretful

for all the things
you had

to let go.

## FELT LIKE

Yes it is true,
I can admit

I fell in love
with you

faster than I should
have,

but I can also admit,
that it took

a lifetime
to get over you...

or at least,
that is what

it felt like.

# FROM THE START

Would you still love me
after all these years

of being apart.

After all these years
of telling ourselves

we weren't meant
to be.

And after all these years
we tried to convince

our hearts
to move on

but failed to let go
because of the things

we felt
from the start.

## THE MOST

You let go
as if

you didn't care
and sadly,

I learned
to move on

as if

I never felt
anything from the start.

And that's
what hurts

the most.

## WOULD YOU HAVE

Would you have told me
you loved me

if you knew
things would eventually

fall apart.

Would you have
kissed me the same.

Laughed with me
the same.

Looked at me
and thought of me

the same.

Would you have
held me

in your arms
that one night

I broke apart.

Would you have cried

the same way
you did

when we let
each other go.

Would you have had it
any different

or would you
relive what we once had

the very same way.

Tell me
how much you miss

what we
once had

and if you ever
wonder

what it would be like
if we decided

to stay.

We've let
so much time

pass us by

and still,
we pretend

like everything is okay,

when we both
clearly know

it is not,
and that's what hurts.

The fact that
we still care,

that we still
love each other,

but not enough
to do something about it.

Not enough
to make things work.

And not enough
to put the past

behind us
and make sense

of all the pain
and dying stars

we've caused.

## THE NIGHT TIME

And yes,
I've let too much

time pass.

I've gone silent
for far too long,

but that doesn't mean
I don't miss you.

That doesn't mean
I don't think of you,

and above all,
that doesn't mean

I don't fight
the urge

to reach out to you—at
night…

when I think of you
the most.

## ANOTHER TRY

What hurts most is,

I know
you're the last person

I should be loving
but it's so hard

to let go.

It's so hard
to say good-bye

and mean it—to
walk away

without giving it
another try.

# I STILL FEEL

And then
they asked me

if I still loved you.

And it's hard to say
but I stayed silent...

because I knew

I shouldn't
be feeling

the things
I still felt.

We all have
a secret somewhere.

Lingering in the back
of our hearts

where all the things
we need…

go.

## OUR OWN

We all have
that one person

we shouldn't be loving.

That one person
who doesn't deserve us.

That one person
we want to save

but can't
because deep down inside

we know
they will never

be ours.

It hurts to say,
but that person

was never
in your grasp

to begin with,

always

a hairline away
but never close enough

to claim
as our own.

*That is just
how it is*

*sometimes.*

## YOU THINK?

You have to understand
that the weather

is going to change.

That sometimes
it's going to get

too cold—too
hot and you might

even drown
when it rains.

It's hard…
but you'll live through it.

You must understand,
that yes,

you're a flower,
but you're also

a lot tougher
than you think.

## BEGIN TO LEAVE

And some people
will hate you

for no apparent reason.

They will hate you
for trying to change

and help
other people's lives.

They will hate you
for your art.

Hate you
for the way you feel.

Hate you
for the way

you love
and the way

you don't love.

They will hate you
for anything,

but most importantly,
they will hate you

for something
they know

they could have done
but didn't

have the heart
to begin

or end.

## NOT NORMAL

Love yourself.

Yes, of course,
because it is easier

said than done.

It is easier
to say

than to practice.

Imagine how hard
it is

when almost everything
we see

is meant
to bring us down.

Every thought,
every chance

and decision
is meant

to break us down.

Imagine this,
living our lives

any different.

Seeing how beautiful
we are from the start.

How beautiful
we could be

without judgment
and guilt

being shoved
in our faces.

*This is where it hurts.*

We are raised to believe
that we aren't special.

That we aren't capable
of being anything

but normal.

## FORGIVE YOURSELF

Because saying it
is one thing

and *knowing* it
with your heart

is another.

So when someone says
you have to love yourself,

yes, of course,
we all know this,

but it is also
something very hard
to do.

It is hard
to live by

what we all
preach,

*"to love yourself."*

So instead of saying this,
I rather say

to try
to love yourself.

To try
to take yourself

and your feelings
under consideration

when presented
with something hard
to do.

And to try,
but not just for me
or yourself,

but for everyone
around you as well.

To try
to be a better person.

To try
to be more open minded
and understanding.

To try
to love others.

To try

to work on yourself.

That is all
it really is, *really*.

To try
to better yourself

as time goes on.

To try
to do something

about all this pain.

To try
to remind yourself

that you are capable
and deserving

of so much more.

That alone
is enough to make a difference

and enough
to save everything

you love...
including yourself.

## BEAUTIFUL HUMAN

There's still time
for you

and there always will be.

Just take
what you have

and make the best
of it.

Take what you have
and make it work.

You're a beautiful human
and you should work

on what matters most.

You should take
what you feel

and go with it.

There's so much time
left for you.

You can still

be

who you want
to become.

Just put the effort in
and make everything

you ever wanted...
yours.

## ISOLATE YOURSELF

Solitude can sometimes
be a gift.

Learn to be
by yourself.

Learn to listen
to your own voice.

*To use it.*
Trust your gut.

Follow your thoughts
and your heart.

Abide by this.
Learn by this.

Isolation
can sometimes be

a blessing.

I'm no preacher
cause preaching

*is not*
what I do.

I just want
to give you

the raw truth.
The ugly truth.

What some of us
don't want to do.

Let go.

It's okay.

Spend some time alone
and realize

how sometimes,
when in the company

of yourself...

you can learn more
about the world

and people
and feelings

than you can ever
learn

in any institution

or school.

You're heart
has all the answers.

All you have to do
is isolate yourself

and pay attention.